A Little Book
of St Pio
of Pietrelcina

Compiled and introduced by

First published in 2003 by
the columba press
55A Spruce Avenue, Stillorgan Industrial Park,
Blackrock, Co Dublin

Designed by Bill Bolger
Origination by The Columba Press
Printed in Ireland by
ColourBooks Ltd, Dublin

ISBN 1 85607 409 9

✝

To
Frank Burke and Shane Redmond
and to the memory of
Gary Burke

Acknowledgements

The publisher and editor gratefully acknowledge the permission of the following to quote from material in their copyright: Edizioni Padre Pio da Pietrelcina for quotations from *Padre Pio of Pietrelcina Letters*, Volumes I, II and III, edited by Melchiorre of Pobladura and Alessandro of Ripabottoni and Fr Gerardo Di Flumeri, OFM Cap (English Version).

✝

Author's Acknowledgements

Sincere thanks are owed to the following for their kind support and assistance with this publication: Fr Peter Rodgers, OFM Cap, Minister Provincial, Fr Christopher Twomey, OFM Cap, and the Capuchin Franciscan Order Council (Ireland) for their very kind support and encouragement; Gary Burke, RIP, who departed this life on 7 March 2003; to Frank Burke and A Gift of Roses Trust for their openness and support; to Bernie Bergin for her assistance with parallel reading and great goodwill, humour and friendship; to John Ryan and his daughter Emer for editorial assistance; to Mario Bruschi, an enthusiastic devotee of Padre Pio, whom I was fortunate to meet at the

✝

St Pio of Pietrelcina Anniversary Liturgical Celebration, at St. Patrick's Cathedral, New York, on 21 September 2002, and who directed me to Padre Pio's letters; to Eileen Maguire and Maureen Hunt of the Irish Office for Padre Pio, Robert Hacker (English Office) and Lorna Cifaldi (The Voice of Padre Pio) San Giovanni for invaluable help and assistance; to Seán O Boyle and the staff of Columba Press; to Sr Madonna Ratliff, FSP and the staff of Pauline Books and Media (USA); Mr Seamus Cashman who planted the seed of this Little Book series; and last but not least, my family: Margaret, Thérèse, Carl and Emma for their continued kindness and warmth.

✝

Introduction

Padre Pio was born on 25 May 1887 to humble farming parents in Pietrelcina, in the south of Italy. All through his life he was plagued by ill health.

At the age of 15 he entered the novitiate of the Franciscan Capuchin Friars and was ordained a priest in 1910. On 20 September 1918 the sacred stigmata appeared on his hands, feet and side. It was a privilege he shared with the founder of the Franciscan Order, St Francis of Assisi.

†

Continual sacrifice and prayer marked Padre Pio's entire life. His letters reveal a man in torment from acute physical and spiritual suffering. At its core, however, was a soul being transformed by the mystical fusion of grace and mercy. Padre Pio embodied human frailty made powerful by a life surrendered to the furnace of God's love. His burning love for the Eucharist and the mother of Jesus made him a magnet for hundreds of thousands of pilgrims who testified to powerful conversions of heart by simply entering his presence, especially in the confessional.

Padre Pio died on 23 September 1968.

✝

Over 100,000 people attended his funeral
and interment in the crypt of Our Lady of
Grace Church, San Giovanni Rotunda.
He was canonised St Pio of Pietrelcina on
16 June 2002 by Pope John Paul II who
announced that his feastday would be the
anniversary of his death.

The following quotations and prayers
allow the reader to encounter one of the
outstanding spiritual leaders of the
twentieth century.

Don Mullan
Dublin
7 April 2003

Quotations from
St Pio
of Pietrelcina

HAPPY THE SOULS

How happy are those souls
who live by faith;
who adore the holy plan
of God in everything,
who rejoice at their afflictions
and convert woodworm to honey.

✝

GOD'S LOVE FOR US

May the Lord have pity on me
and since he loves me so much,
may he make me capable
of doing something for his glory.

†

Oh, what a wonderful thing it is
to become a victim of divine love!

✝

My heart has found at last
a Lover so attached to me
that I am incapable
of hurting him any more.

✝

GOD'S LOVE FOR US

My soul yearns to be consumed
by the flame of that intense love
which destroys without causing pain.

† _____

GOD'S LOVE FOR US

I feel again the love of my God
rising up like a giant in my poor heart.
I still have the confidence and the strength
to cry aloud with St Peter:
Lord, save me, I am perishing!

✝

OUR LOVE OF GOD

It can all be summed up as follows:
I am consumed by love for God
and love for my neighbour.

✝

OUR LOVE OF GOD

I'd like to fly off
to invite all creatures
to love Jesus and Mary.

OUR LOVE OF GOD

I feel very keenly the desire
to spend every moment of my life
in loving the Lord.
I would like to hold his hand very tightly
and run joyful along the painful road
on which he has placed me.

OUR LOVE OF GOD

God is continually fixed in my mind
and imprinted on my heart.
I never lose sight of him.

OUR LOVE OF GOD

Pardon me.
It is a man madly in love with his God
who is speaking to you
and deserves your pity.

✝

OUR LOVE OF GOD

God …
absolutely cannot reject
the sincere desire to love him.

†

LIFE

I always have before my mental gaze
the clear knowledge that
only by death is true life to be found.

LIFE

Instead of frightening me,
death is the most ardent desire
of my heart,
the summit of my happiness.

THE DAWN

I await the dawn,
because my weak sight
couldn't bear the brilliance of the sun.

The Kiss of Peace

He will come to take us in his arms
and give us the kiss of peace
in the last sacraments
at the hour of death.
Thus we shall end our life
in the holy kiss of the Lord.

Pain and Suffering

I must admit that I am happy
even in the midst of these afflictions
because almost every day
our good Jesus
also makes me taste great sweetness.

†

PAIN AND SUFFERING

What is my suffering
in comparison to
what I deserve for my sins?

Pain and Suffering

Love is the first ingredient
in the relief of suffering.

✝

FAITH

Even to say *I believe*
is for me an atrocious torment …
What bitter pain remains
in the depths of my soul
which is gradually being withdrawn
from created light
without perceiving any other light!

GOD'S WILL

I feel within me
the great need to cry out
louder and louder to Jesus
with the doctor of grace:
Give me what you command,
and command what you will.

GOD'S WILL

My poor soul,
crushed by sorrow
and with no more strength left,
turns to the Lord and says:
Not my will, O most sweet Jesus,
but thine be done ...

✝

GOD'S WILL

Nothing is due to me.
I am an instrument in divine hands;
an instrument which only succeeds
in serving some purpose
when it is handled by
the divine Craftsman.
Left to my own devices, I can do nothing
but sin ... and sin again.

✝

PEACE

Peace is simplicity of heart,
serenity of mind,
tranquillity of soul,
the bond of love.

PEACE

Peace is the way to perfection;
indeed in peace is perfection to be found.

PEACE

If we keep our souls calm and peaceful
in every difficult situation,
we will gain much ground
in the ways of God.

JUDGING PEOPLE

Be careful, above all,
of charity towards God,
your neighbour and yourself.
Refrain from judging anyone whomsoever,
except when it is your duty to do so.

JUDGING PEOPLE

In this way
you will hold everyone in esteem
and you will also show yourself
to be a worthy son of the heavenly Father.

SPIRITUAL STRUGGLES

My soul must endure a continual combat.
I see no other way out
than to abandon myself
in the arms of Jesus
where he often allows me to fall asleep.
Blessed sleep!
Happy refreshment for the soul
in the struggles it endures.

✝

SPIRITUAL STRUGGLES

I live in a perpetual night
and this night shows
no sign of withdrawing its thick darkness
to give place to the beautiful dawn.

Sin

A man who fears to offend God
does not in reality offend him,
but he offends him
when this fear ceases.

✝

I should prefer death
a thousand times
rather than deliberately offend
such a good God.

SAVING SOULS

I am ready for anything
as long as Jesus is happy
and will save the souls
of my brothers and sisters,
especially those
he has entrusted to my care.

Saving Souls

Don't worry about stealing my time,
because the best way
of spending one's time ... is to spend it
in furthering the salvation
and sanctification of others.

✝

Confidence

In this torment of the heart
I feel greater confidence in God
and I am so filled with sorrow for my sins
that I endure a continual martyrdom.

✝

SAD TIMES

These are very sad times,
but what can be done?
O unfortunate times
on which we have fallen!

✝

ANGELS

The heavenly beings continue to visit me
and to give me a foretaste
of the rapture of the blessed.
While the mission of our
guardian angels is a great one,
my own angel's mission
is certainly greater,
since he has the additional task
of teaching me other languages.

✝

HUMILITY

Far from considering myself
better than others, I believe instead
that of all those on earth
I am the one who serves the Lord least.
By means of this grace
he has given me such a clear view
that I see myself obliged
more than anyone else to love my Creator.

HUMILITY

Humble yourself before the Lord
with complete confidence
and don't be afraid by any means,
for no harm will come to you.

HUMILITY

Be humble with others
since God opposes the proud
and gives grace to the humble.

HUMILITY

God speaks to those who are humble.

✝

I SUFFER GREATLY

I suffer greatly when I see
how people ignore Jesus,
and what is worse,
how they even insult him,
especially by those dreadful blasphemies.
I should like to die,
or at least become deaf
rather than hear so many insults
offered to God by men.

LET ME DIE

I have prayed to the Lord as follows:
Lord, let me die
rather than be present
when people are offending you!

IN EXILE

I am aware of being in exile
along with many other souls,
but suffer immensely to see
how few of these aspire
like myself
to the Promised Land.

THE CROSS

May the Cross always be our bed of rest,
our school of perfection,
our beloved heritage.
For this reason we must never separate
the Cross from Jesus' love;
otherwise it would become a weight,
which in our weakness we could not carry.

✝

THE CROSS

I don't desire by any means
to have my cross lightened,
since I am happy to suffer with Jesus.
In contemplating the Cross
on his shoulders
I feel more and more fortified
and I exult with a holy joy.

THE CROSS

I know from my own experience
that the best way to avoid falling
is to lean on the Cross of Jesus,
with confidence in him alone
who for our salvation
desired to be nailed to it.

THE CROSS

How unbearable is pain
when suffered far from the Cross,
but how sweet and bearable it becomes
when it is offered
close to the Cross of Jesus!

THE DEVIL

I am right in the grip of the devil
who is trying with all his might
to snatch me from the hands of Jesus.
I am alone in this combat
and my heart is filled with terror.
What is to become of me I do not know.
I feel very weak in mind and body,
Father,
but I abandon myself in God's hands.

✝

The Devil

Our enemy plots against us
but despise him in the name of Jesus
and laugh heartily at him.
This is the best way
to make him beat a retreat.

✝

THE DEVIL

I had a very bad time the night before last;
from about ten o'clock,
when I went to bed,
until five o'clock in the morning
that wretch
did nothing but beat me continually.

✝

THE DEVIL

He presented to my mind
many diabolical suggestions,
thoughts of despair,
distrust in God.
But praise be to Jesus,
for I defended myself
by saying to him repeatedly:
your wounds are my merit.

✝

FEAR NOT

Do not fear the enemy;
he will not launch anything
against the little ship of your spirit
because Jesus is the helmsman
and Mary is the star.

Fight Valiantly

Let the enemy wage war on you,
but he will never be able to bite you.
Fight valiantly;
always struggle against
the appetites of the flesh,
against worldly vanity,
against the seduction of gold or dignity,
with which the devil
continually wages war on us.

GOD'S CLOSENESS

Be firmly convinced
that the more the assaults
of the enemy increase,
the closer God is to the soul.
Think of and ponder well
this great and comforting truth.

✝

Heavenly Support

Jesus, our dear Mother, my little angel,
St Joseph and our father, St Francis,
are almost always with me.

CONSCIENCE

I have been troubled continually
in conscience
on the score of my past life,
so badly spent.
I need some help that will calm
the surging waves in my soul,
for, believe me; this is the thought
which is killing me.

CONSCIENCE

Never lie down to sleep
without having first
examined your conscience
on the way you have spent the day
and without first turning your thoughts
to God.

✝

To receive Jesus

May all be for the glory of Jesus.
How could I live, my dear Father,
if I were to fail
even for a single morning
to receive Jesus?

THE BLESSED SACRAMENT

I can only say that when I am close
to Jesus in the Blessed Sacrament
my heart throbs so violently
that it seems to me at times
that it must burst out of my chest.

✝

The Blessed Sacrament

You do well to desire to be united
with him every day
and the best proof of this is that,
whenever you can,
you never neglect to go to Jesus
in the Blessed Sacrament
to give and receive the kiss of peace.

†

COMMUNION

Only the certainty
that you are in a state of mortal sin
should keep you from Communion.
When in doubt, make an act of contrition
and receive Communion.
Do this under obedience
and this holds good always
and at all times.

✝

LOVE

Don't refuse in any way or for any reason
to act charitably to all without exception.
Go out of your way to do this
when you get the chance.
The Lord desires it
and you must make an effort to do it.

✝

LOVE

What I understand most truly and clearly
is that my heart loves
to a much greater extent
than my intellect perceives.

LOVE

How happy is the interior kingdom,
    when holy love reigns there!
How blessed are the faculties of the soul
    when they obey so wise a king!

LOVE

When fear and love are united,
they help each other, like sisters,
to remain on their feet
and to walk securely in the Lord's paths.

LOVE

Love makes us hasten with rapid strides
while fear, on the other hand,
makes us watch prudently
where we place our feet
and guides us so that
we may never stumble
on the road leading to heaven.

✝

LOVE

Let us be very fond of charity
and let us practise it.
This is the virtue
that makes us all children
of the one Father who is in heaven.

GOD'S GLORY

May the divine plan
be accomplished in me
as long as it is
for the glory of our dear Jesus.

✝

GOD'S GLORY

I know one thing for certain,
that this good is inexhaustible
and not circumscribed by limits.
I understand moreover, that …
this is a very great good,
an immense good,
an infinite good.
Is this Jesus?
If not, then who is it?

PRESENCE OF JESUS

Where Jesus is,
there can neither be defeat
nor anything that displeases him.

JOY AND HAPPINESS

People cannot understand
that when paradise is poured into a heart,
[it] cannot bear it without weeping ...
it was the joy that filled my heart,
which caused me to weep for so long.

JOY AND HAPPINESS

This vision and locution of Our Lord
plunged my soul into such peace
and happiness
that all the sweetnesses of the world
appear tasteless in comparison
to even a single drop of this bliss.

JOY AND HAPPINESS

Nothing can dry up
and actually does dry up
the milk and honey of charity
like regrets, affliction and melancholy.
Live, then, in holy joy ...

Heavenly Mother

In my greatest sufferings
it seems to me
that I no longer have a mother
on this earth,
but a very compassionate one in heaven.

✝

BELOVED MOTHER

I now seem to understand the martyrdom
of our most beloved Mother …
Oh, if people would only fathom
this martyrdom!
Who would fail to sympathise
with this dear co-redemptrix of ours?
Who would deny her the beautiful title
'Queen of Martyrs'?

✝

BLESSED MOTHER

We must make every effort
to follow invariably this Blessed Mother,
to walk close to her
since there is no other path
leading to life
except the path followed by our Mother.

✝

MORE THAN I ASK

He has never refused me anything
and indeed I must say
he has given me more than I asked.

✝

May Jesus be forever praised,
for he never withdraws his mercy
from me!

✝

IMMORTAL YOUTH

May Jesus bless you and comfort you
and may he one day introduce you
into the splendour of his immortal youth.

PRAYER

Let us pray to our most merciful Jesus
to come to the aid of his Church,
for her needs have become extreme.

✝

PRAYER

May Our Lord be always with you
and make you holy.

PRAYER

May the Holy Spirit fill you
with his most holy gifts,
may he sanctify you,
guide you along the path
to eternal salvation
and comfort you
in your innumerable troubles.

† _____

Prayer

Pray and ask the heavenly Spouse
never to allow this harsh northerly wind
to blow over the little garden of your soul,
but to deign in his compassion as Lover
to send invariably the south wind
which is the only one
capable of awakening chaste and holy love.

PRAYER

Say to yourself,
if I have not lived well in the past
I intend to live well in the future,
with the divine assistance.

✝

PRAYER

The only way to gain your health [of soul]
is through prayer;
you cannot win the battle without prayer.

Morning Praises

I sleep with a smile of sweet beatitude
on my lips
and a perfectly tranquil countenance,
waiting for a little companion
of my childhood to come to waken me,
so that we may sing together
the morning praises
to the Beloved of our hearts.

†

Jesus makes us so happy on earth,
what will heaven be like?

HEAVEN

Only in heaven will everything be
spring as regards beauty;
autumn as regards enjoyment
and summer as regards love.
There will be no winter,
but here winter is necessary
in order to practice abnegation
and those beautiful little virtues,
which are practised in time of sterility.

✝

THE HOLY SPIRIT

Never fall back on yourself alone,
but place all your trust in God ...
Let the Holy Spirit act within you.
Give yourself up to all his transports
and have no fear.
He is so wise and gentle and discreet
that he never brings about anything
but good.

THE HOLY SPIRIT

How good this Holy Spirit,
this Comforter, is to all,
but how supremely good he is
to those who seek him!

† —

TRUST

Your soul is in the arms
of your divine Spouse,
like a baby in its mother's arms.
You may sleep in peace therefore,
for this heavenly Spouse will guide you
in the way which is
to your greatest advantage.

TRUST

Take courage, you are quite safe,
for God is with you.
What then, have you to fear?
Allow yourself to be led
by divine grace and be at peace,
for he will be glorified in you.

TRUST

In order to reach our final goal,
we must follow our divine Leader,
who usually leads chosen souls
by the path he himself has trodden
and by no other.

✝

Trust

Be firm in your resolutions,
stay in the boat
in which Jesus has placed you
and let the storm come.

The soul and God

My whole soul ... gravitates towards God
with a marvellous impetus and readiness,
and what is more surprising,
the soul itself is unaware
of this movement.

The soul and God

I am also seized by a great desire
to serve God with perfection.
There is then no torment
that my soul would not joyfully suffer.

✝

GOD'S MERCY

The bitterness of the trial is sweetened
by the balm of God's goodness and mercy.

GOD'S MERCY

The thought of God's mercy
is the only thing that sustains me.

✝

GOD'S MERCY

I don't know how to thank
the heavenly Father for his mercy
when he introduces souls to me
to whom I can be helpful in some way.

†

SIMPLICITY

Jesus likes to give himself to simple souls;
we must make an effort to acquire
this beautiful virtue of simplicity
and to hold it in great esteem.

✝

Your troubles

I feel all your troubles
as if they were my own.

✝

TEMPTATION

The more fully you become
the friend and intimate of God,
the more you will have
to endure temptation.
Temptation is a most convincing proof
that God is united with a soul:
I will be with him in trouble.

TEMPTATION

I understand that temptations
seem to stain rather than purify the soul,
but this is not really the case.
It suffices to know
what the great St Francis de Sales says,
namely, that temptations are like the soap
which when spread on the laundry
seems to soil but in reality cleanses it.

✝

TEMPTATION

The Lord is faithful.
He never allows you to be tempted
beyond your strength.
You must be strong and cheerful in spirit,
for the Lord is
in the depths of your heart.

TEMPTATION

Temptation is a sure sign
that the soul is very pleasing to the Lord.

✝

GOD'S GOODNESS

I have no adequate words
by which to thank the Lord
for his goodness.

✝

GOD'S GOODNESS

Oh! If we could only perceive
for a single instant
that which still amazes
the heavenly spirits themselves, namely,
the state to which God's grace
has raised us,
to be nothing less than his own children,
destined to reign with his Son
for all eternity!

†

GOD'S GOODNESS

Blessed Jesus! What a lot he has to bear
from this rebel son of his!
If he were anyone but himself,
he would have cast me off long ago!
How patient this Jesus is!
How good he is to everyone
but more especially to me.

†

GOD'S GOODNESS

Oh how good God is.
It is true that he is good to all,
but he is particularly good to those
who place all their trust in him.

CONVERSION

I am seeking the amendment of my life,
my spiritual resurrection,
true and substantial love,
the sincere conversion
of my whole self to him.

Conversion

Dear God!
Bring me to repentance,
constrain me to sincere contrition
and resolute conversion
of my heart to you.

SPIRITUAL IMPROVEMENT

We are never done trying
to improve our appearance.
Indeed, all our efforts are directed towards
improving the body
and making it more and more beautiful.
Less attention is perhaps devoted
to the soul,
which we may have treated
as a negligible quantity.

SPIRITUAL IMPROVEMENT

God in his infinite wisdom
has placed in our hands
all the necessary means
for the embellishment of our souls,
even after we have disfigured them by sin.

Spiritual improvement

Walk always, even if slowly;
you will make progress just the same.

Spiritual Improvement

When you are unable to take big steps
on the path along which God leads you,
patiently wait until your legs
are strong enough to run,
or rather, until you have the wings to fly.

✝

Faith, Hope and Love

I desire no greater pleasure
than my faith, my hope, my love;
to be able only to say sincerely,
even if sometimes without feeling,
that I would rather die
than abandon this virtue.